ACKNOWLEDGMENTS

As is the case with so many creative endeavors, the inspiration and help of a good number of people have gone into each page of this book.

I especially owe much to my wife, Michele Montez, not only for her beautiful illustrations but for her shared appreciation of wild plants and of nature as a whole as well. I speak for her also in offering much thanks to our family and friends for their support and encouragement.

Thanks are due to John Javna for his valuable help and shared knowledge in many areas, and to Joe Hartman also, for his support and genuine enthusiasm.

I'm grateful to Megan Hiller, Rick Newby, Kathy Springmeyer, Dana Kim, and everyone at Falcon Press as well.

C O N T E N T S

About This Book

The book you hold in your hand was created with a definite purpose in mind. It is, as the title states, an introduction to common edible and useful wild plants and is designed to be a practical handbook for beginners.

There are many books in print today dealing with the subject of wild plant identification in North America. While some address a wide variety of plant species found throughout much of the continent, others focus only on specific regional identification. For the beginner, such books can be overwhelming in terms of the amount of botanical information provided and in the extensive volumes of plants identified. Additionally, in the case of many of the smaller regional guides, the illustrations or photographs are often vague.

Willow Bark & Rosehips outlines thirty of the more common wild plants of North America. All are clearly illustrated in full color. A good number of the species identified can be found in both urban and rural environments. The various plant descriptions are brief but informative, and the language in the identifying text is deliberately common, avoiding as much as possible the use of the scientific or botanical terminology. You will see "spp." used when several closely related species fit the descriptive and usage information given. In such cases, a representative of that genus or plant group is pictured.

Therefore, with this book in hand and the desire to spend a bit of time exploring, it should be possible for a beginner to easily identify and enjoy the benefits of many plants found growing in the wild.

*O*n a cold autumn day some 5,000 years ago, a tired traveler paused on his journey through the high mountains of central Europe, resting at an altitude of more than 10,000 feet. He was hiking through a pass in the Alps, near what is now the border between Austria and Italy.

Although the high mountain air was uncomfortably cold, the traveler was well protected. His clothing of finely patchworked animal skins helped retain body heat, while a thick cape of dry, bundled grasses provided additional warmth. His feet were protected by leather shoes lined with dry grass for extra comfort and insulation.

As he sat down to rest, the sky turned white and snow began to fall heavily. He could still make out the brilliant autumn foliage lining a valley thousands of feet below. In his home village, his family and friends waited by a warm fire, and wondered. They waited for days, then weeks, but he never returned.

On a September day in 1991, two hikers found the traveler's body encased in ice, undisturbed for 5,000 years. His body, clothing, and numerous tools and other artifacts were surprisingly well preserved.

Objects found with the "ice man," as he is known, are not only fascinating, but provide valuable knowledge of how humans have utilized wild plants throughout history. Creative use of plants for food, clothing, shelter, and medicine has sustained humankind for countless generations. The ice man helps us realize our historic link to the world of wild plants.

Many of the plants he utilized can be found throughout North America today. For instance, he carried a birch bark container filled with bits of charcoal wrapped in green leaves. A strong glue made from the gum of a birch tree was used to bind his ax. His backpack frame was made of hazelnut and larch woods, and his flint knife, with a handle of ash, was found lying next to its sheath of woven grass. He carried a length of rope, also of woven grass, and a longbow crafted of flexible wood from the yew tree.

The ice man's knowledge of wild plants and their many uses was central to his existence.

Although this precious knowledge appears to be rapidly fading in contemporary society, it is by no means entirely lost.

Throughout North America, and in other parts of the world, a practical knowledge of edible and useful wild plants can still be found. A broad range of wild plant—related practices are inherent in the continuing cultures of many indigenous peoples.

The art and craft of fine basketry, for example, is still widely enjoyed. Willows, Cattails, grasses, roots, and a variety of other useful plant fibers are still the mainstays of basket construction.

The practical and spiritual values of important medicinal plants are also known and appreciated. Wild plants are the source of many modern pharmaceuticals, and traditional herbal remedies continue to be respected.

The nutritional and culinary value of wild plants has been recognized for centuries. Today, the curiosity and renewed interest in gathering wild edibles links us, in part, to the ways of those who have come before us.

Plants that were important to our ancestors now grow abundantly in vacant lots, along country roads, and in the cracks of city streets and sidewalks. The seeds of an extremely common wild plant known as Lamb's Quarters (see page 28) have been unearthed by archaeologists at Neolithic dwelling sites. Evidence of the use of Plantain (see page 44), another abundant wild plant, has been found in the tombs of ancient Egypt, and the highly nutritious Amaranth (see page 10), long used and appreciated by humans, now grows wild throughout much of North America. The seeds of our past are literally among us.

We *can* rekindle our time—honored relationship with all that is natural, and discovering the treasures growing right at our feet is a good place to start. To reclaim a knowledge of wild plants is to gain a new/old sense of our very existence and to wonder at the history of our intimate bond.

H A B I T A T

*A*maranthus retroflexus, and
other closely related Amaranths,
will grow in a wide range of
environments, including
roadsides, fields,
vacant lots, near
sidewalks and
trails, and along
walls and fences.

Amaranthus retroflexus

*O*f the 30 or more species of Amaranths growing throughout North America, Green Amaranth (*Amaranthus retroflexus*), also known as *Redroot Pigweed*, is one of the most common. It generally grows at elevations below 7,500 feet.

The leaves of this valuable plant are oval and pointed, medium green on top, and lighter green with prominent veins underneath. The feathery and somewhat prickly flower heads appear from summer through autumn at the junctions of stalks and leaf stems, and in clusters along the upper portions of the plants. Green Amaranth matures at a height of several inches to 5 feet, but often forms seeds when 1 to 3 feet tall.

U S A G E

* The seeds, often available in large quantities, are one of this plant's greatest values.

* When lightly roasted or parched, these nutritious, tiny, dark seeds can be used in a variety of ways (see pages 75-76). Finely ground, they make an excellent grain meal. When cooked whole with water, the seeds produce a delicious cereal mush, which can be eaten hot, or dried into flour.

* The raw young leaves are good in salads and, like the older leaves, can be cooked like spinach. These greens, which in some areas can be collected year-round in abundance, are a very good source of vitamins A and C. Because they tend to be mild flavored, Amaranth leaves are a good addition to some of the stronger flavored wild greens such as Curly Dock, Wild Mustard, and Dandelion.

Indigenous peoples of the Americas have cultivated Amaranths for many centuries, and they are now grown and harvested commercially.

Cattail

Typha spp.

H A B I T A T

Cattails grow in or near streams, rivers, ponds, lakes, marshes, and wetlands.

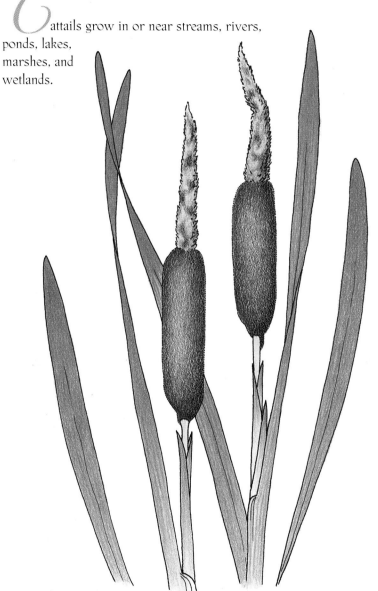

Typha latifolia

*T*he common Broad-leaved Cattail *(Typha latifolia)* and other closely related species grow throughout much of North America and in many parts of Europe and Asia, usually at elevations below 8,000 feet.

This well-known plant, with its long, narrow, sword-shaped leaves, grows 2 ½ to 10 feet tall. The spiked brown flower heads appear from late spring through autumn. Plants grow in patches of only a few to acres of many thousands.

USAGE

❦ The young shoots, 4 to 16 inches long, cut from the rootstalks and with the outer leaves peeled away, are the tender, edible portion of the plant. You can eat these shoots raw or add them to any variety of salad. They are also good steamed, boiled, or sautéed and can be used in dishes calling for cooked vegetables.

❦ During their growing season, cattails produce a fine, yellow pollen along the upper portion of each central flower stalk. This occurs throughout the spring or into summer, depending on regional conditions. If numerous plants are available, you can collect pollen by shaking the flower heads into a paper or plastic bag, without uprooting any plants. Further shaking the pollen in a can or other container brings small insects and debris to the surface for removal.

❦ Cattail pollen makes delicious pancakes, especially when blended with equal amounts of whole-grain flour. This pollen is a good addition to breads, cakes, and muffins, and to any number of other wild-food recipes.

❦ In late summer and autumn, you can collect the dry flower heads and gently undo them by rubbing them apart into a good-sized bag or sack. This natural down makes a soft stuffing for such items as pillows and quilts.

The long leaves are traditionally used for weaving mats, baskets,
and the seats of handcrafted chairs.

H A B I T A T

This adaptable native of Europe and Asia grows, often in abundance, throughout much of North America, along highways and other road-sides, and in vacant lots and open fields.

Cichorium intybus

*T*he erect, branching stems of this hearty wild plant, also known as *Wild Succory* or *Blue Sailors*, grow 1 to 4 feet high. A rosette–patterned base of dandelion–like leaves appears in the spring, with smaller, simpler greens developing later along the upper stems. When it blooms, from late spring through autumn, you can identify Chicory by its beautiful, sky blue flowers, which open early in the morning and often close by midday.

U S A G E

❧ You can collect and eat the entire young plant in the spring. The tender leaves make a great addition to salads. As the plants mature, the older leaves are best steamed or boiled; add them to any dish calling for cooked greens.

❧ The dried and roasted roots of Chicory can be ground and brewed into a rich-flavored beverage, considered by many to be an excellent coffee substitute *(see pages 71 and 76)*. These dark-roasted roots have long been a main ingredient in New Orleans style coffee blends.

❧ The dried or roasted roots make a good addition to wild-tea blends.

Chicory Tea:
- $1/4$ cup chopped Chicory root, dried or dried and roasted (the roasted root will have a stronger flavor)
- 1 cup Wild Strawberry leaves, dried and crushed
- 1 cup Stinging Nettle leaves, dried and crushed

Combine and steep the ingredients to desired strength.

This lovely plant, grown and harvested commercially for its roots and greens, is rich in vitamins A and C.

Chokecherry

Prunus spp.

H A B I T A T

Chokecherry trees grow well in a variety of climates and habitats, including open and mixed woodlands, canyons, and hillsides. They are common along creeks, streams, and rivers.

Prunus virginiana

*T*hese deciduous fruit trees native to North America have brown to red–brown bark and grow 3 to 45 feet high.

Flowers of different species appear in spring and range from white to pink–red. Fruits ripen from late summer through autumn and range in color from bright red to deep purple. The rich green leaves are pointed, are oval to oblong, and have serrated edges.

U S A G E

- Chokecherry fruit, sometimes called *Stone Fruit* or *Wild Cherry,* has a unique flavor and makes delicious jellies, jams, syrups, and puddings.

- You can collect these small cherries through late autumn. They remain quite good after the fruit has dried a bit on the tree.

- Traditionally, indigenous peoples of North America have mixed the dried and ground fruit with meats and other foods.

- The fruits can be fresh-frozen or stored dry. Remove pits by pushing simmered fruit pulp through a coarse strainer or sieve.

- The special flavor of this native fruit makes it a valued addition to any number of foods, wild or otherwise.

- Chokecherry is one of the most widely distributed trees in North America, due in part, perhaps, to the large number of birds and other animals that eat the cherries.

☞ *Caution: Chokecherry leaves and pits contain a cyanide toxin that is rendered harmless by drying or cooking. The fruit pits, whole or ground, should not be eaten unless cooked or thoroughly dried.*

Cow Parsnip

Heracleum lanatum

HABITAT

*C*ow Parsnip is widespread throughout North America in moist environments, often in woodlands and along creeks, streams, and rivers.

Heracleum lanatum

Also known as *Wild Rhubarb*, Cow Parsnip grows 3 to 8 feet tall. Thick, grooved, branching stalks and stems produce large, generally 3-parted leaves that are coarsely toothed and prominently veined. In spring, small white flowers appear at the ends of stalks in umbrella-like clusters known as umbels.

U S A G E

- You can collect the young leaf stalks and flower stems in spring, before the flowers mature. Cut them into small pieces and boil or stew until tender.

- Cow Parsnip root is easily dug with a trowel. Add it to soups, stews, and other cooked dishes.

- If the plant flavor is too strong or bitter, change the water once or twice while cooking. Cow Parsnip can be mixed with milder flavored greens such as Amaranth *(see page 10)*, Lamb's Quarters *(see page 28)*, or the leaves of Stinging Nettle *(see page 38)*, which often grows nearby.

- Cow Parsnip foliage offers a special and rare feature in the realm of wild edibles. The dried leaves, roasted or burned, produce an ash that can be used as a salt substitute.

- Cow Parsnip sap can cause skin irritation after exposure to sunlight. Wear long sleeves and gloves while collecting.

Caution: Deadly poisonous species of Hemlock plants resemble Cow Parsnip in certain growth stages but are easily distinguished by their lack of large leaves. Take great care when collecting and using Cow Parsnip.

Curly Dock

Rumex crispus

HABITAT

Curly Dock grows on open and disturbed ground, such as in vacant lots, fields and pastures, and along roads.

Rumex crispus

Curly Dock, also known as *Yellow Dock*, is part of a large sorrel family that has many edible varieties. It is common throughout North America and occurs from sea level to elevations of at least 9,000 feet.

Curly Dock grows 1 to 3 feet tall, with the largest leaves near the base of the plant. These oblong or lancelike leaves have curled or wavy edges.

In late summer and autumn, numerous clusters of small, three-winged seeds cover the main stems, and most of the plant turns a rusty, reddish brown.

USAGE

- Of the many sorrels and docks growing throughout North America, this abundant plant is one of the finest edibles.

- You can gather the tender leaves of any size in substantial quantities from spring through autumn or year-round in some areas. These plants have a pleasant, sour quality and are very tender when cooked. Serve with a little butter and pepper or add to any dish calling for cooked greens.

- Curly Dock, high in vitamins A and C, has long been valued as an herbal medicine. The root is used to treat skin disorders and is said to benefit the liver, kidneys, and bladder.

- This root is also the source of a good yellow dye *(see page 74)*. You can collect the root throughout the year, but it is most potent in autumn.

Caution: Curly Dock leaves can be high in oxalic acid and can cause liver damage in some people. They should not be eaten in large amounts on a daily basis.

H A B I T A T

andelions grow throughout North America and much of the world in a wide variety of habitats, from sea level to elevations of 10,000 feet. They are common in vacant lots, meadows, pastures, and well-groomed lawns.

Taraxacum officinale

*T*he main stem of this well-known plant is hollow, stands 2 to 20 inches tall, and grows from a base rosette of deeply serrated or coarsely toothed, oblong, green leaves. The yellow flower heads that appear at the tops of individual stalks ripen into delicate, white seed-puffs as the plants mature.

U S A G E

❧ Young leaves are well known as a salad green but are also good cooked like spinach. If the leaves taste bitter, cook them with milder tasting greens or change the water once or twice during cooking. The bitter flavor tends to increase as the plants mature.

❧ Roots can be eaten raw, steamed, boiled, or roasted.

❧ When dried and roasted, the roots make a good addition to any number of wild-tea blends and, like Chicory root, produce a fine, coffeelike beverage. Many commercial coffee substitutes include roasted and ground Dandelion root *(see pages 71 and 76)*.

❧ Dandelions, grown commercially for foods and beverages, are also used in modern herbal medicines.

❧ Herbalists have used the fresh or dried root to treat liver and urinary disorders. Dandelion root tea is said to be a powerful diuretic and digestive aid.

❧ Dandelion flowers are the main ingredient in a popular wine and are also a good source for a light yellow dye *(see page 74)*.

Dandelions contain valuable amounts
of vitamins A and C.

Sambucus cerulea

H A B I T A T

*E*lderberry trees grow in moist habitats throughout North America, often along creeks, streams, and rivers.

Sambucus cerulea

*A*lso known as *Elder* or *Blue Elderberry*, this beautiful native tree grows from bush size to 25 feet tall. The long, pointed leaves are serrated and grow opposite each other along single stems. Elderberry trees generally bloom in late spring and early summer, bearing large clusters of white or creamy white flowers. The many-clustered berries ripen from late summer through autumn. They are deep blue and are often covered with a light blue powder.

U S A G E

❦ The small fruits have long been valued as the main ingredient in a popular wine. They make excellent pies, tarts, jellies, jams, sauces, and preserves.

❦ The juice is rich in vitamins A and C and makes a soothing, delicious syrup.

Elderberry Syrup

– Combine 4 cups of Elderberries and 3 cups of water in a pot.
– Bring to a boil slowly, reduce heat, and simmer gently for 10 to 15 minutes.
– Remove from heat and carefully strain. Be sure to crush the pulp through the strainer to extract as much juice as possible, avoiding any inclusion of skins.
– Add $1/2$ cup honey or sugar, more or less to taste, and reheat. (The juice of one small lemon may be added if desired.)
– Simmer gently, uncovered, for 15 to 20 minutes.
– Remove from heat and bottle when cool.

❦ The flower blossoms and berries, fresh or dried, make delicious tea.

❦ Sections of straight Elderberry branches, with the soft inner pith removed, are a good material for making musical flutes.

☞ *Caution: The sometimes bitter skins of the berries can cause serious stomach upset if eaten raw, and the roots are poisonous. Also, avoid the poisonous fruit of the Red Elderberry; its berries are red, not blue.*

H A B I T A T

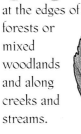

azelnut trees grow throughout North America, often in or at the edges of forests or mixed woodlands and along creeks and streams.

Corylus cornuta

*W*ild Hazelnuts grow from shrub size to 30 feet tall and have smooth, brown to red-brown bark. These deciduous North American trees have serrated, somewhat furry leaves that are round to round-oval and pointed. The small fruits, also known as *Filberts*, generally appear in pairs or groups of three and are encased in prickly green sheaths. These ripen to shades of brown as the nuts mature in summer and autumn.

USAGE

- You can gather the delicious nuts from late summer through autumn. They are a wild version of the commercially grown *Filbert*.

- Although eagerly sought by a variety of animals, these nuts can often be gathered in substantial quantities. If they are beyond reach, try gently shaking them loose or tap them free with a long pole or branch. *(The fine sheath hairs make painful slivers. Wear gloves when collecting Hazelnuts.)*

- The shelled nutmeats can be eaten raw or roasted, or used for making a fine Hazelnut flour *(see pages 75-76)*. If kept dry, the nuts can be stored in their shells for a reasonably long time.

- Hazelnut wood is strong and lightweight. Traditionally, it has been used for arrow shafts.

- You can use the branches in projects requiring a durable, lightweight framework, and they make sturdy canes and walking sticks.

To ensure the health of any Hazelnut tree, prune selectively, removing only a few branches.

HABITAT

This highly useful plant grows throughout North America, along roads and sidewalks, in fields and vacant lots.

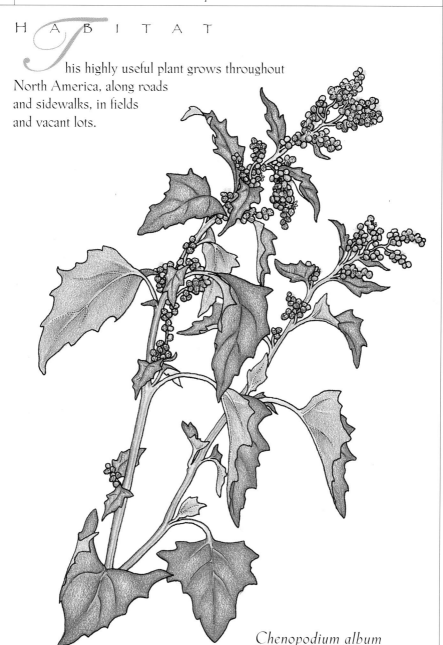

Chenopodium album

*A*lso known as *Goosefoot* or *Wild Spinach,* this common plant grows from several inches to 5 feet tall. The leaves are wedge to egg shaped, with toothed edges. They most often appear powdery, especially their undersides. The bulk of this plant is erect and branching, with small seeds developing in dense clusters at the junctions of leaves and stems.

U S A G E

- You can gather the mild-flavored leaves throughout much of the year in many areas. They are good eaten raw in salads and are delicious cooked like spinach. In fact, Lamb's Quarters is closely related to spinach and other cultivated food plants, including beets and chard.

- The tiny seeds, frequently abundant, are available from late spring through autumn and throughout winter in some areas.

- Large quantities of these seeds can be gathered at once, making them an excellent source of wild-seed meal or flour *(see pages 75-76)*.

- The seeds are also good cooked whole as a hot cereal, or added to breads, muffins, and cakes.

- Lamb's Quarters seed flour, mixed with equal parts of whole wheat flour, makes buckwheatlike pancakes.

This valuable plant, rich in vitamins A and C, has been used by humans for thousands of years. The nutritious seeds are a favorite food of many wild birds and can be collected and used as birdseed.

HABITAT

Mallows are widely distributed and frequently grow in fields and vacant lots, along roads and sidewalks.

Malva parviflora

*A*lso known as *Cheeses* or *Cheeseweed*, this common plant grows 6 inches to 3 feet tall, often in bushlike clusters low to the ground. The fuzzy, green leaves have 5 to 7 lobes, are somewhat round, and resemble those of geraniums. The small, 5-petaled flowers range from white to pink, often tinged with shades of blue.

Several other closely related and edible species of Mallows grow throughout North America. The plant known as *Cheeses*, *M. parviflora*, gets its name from the numerous clusters of seeds it produces that slightly resemble small rounds of cheese.

U S A G E

❦ Raw young leaves, although a bit fuzzy, are quite good in salads. Older greens are best steamed or boiled. Leaves are often available in large quantities and can be added to dishes calling for cooked greens.

❦ With their outer husks removed, the round, green seed clusters can be eaten raw in salads or cooked, husks and all, in soups, stews, and other cooked dishes.

❦ Traditional medicines have long used Mallow leaves and roots. The fresh or dried leaves produce a flavorful tea that is said to soothe coughs and sore throats if sipped warm, *not hot*. The fresh or dried root is similarly beneficial.

Mallow root tea is also used as a soothing herbal treatment for kidney, bladder, and other urinary tract disorders.

Mugwort

Artemisia vulgaris

HABITAT

*T*his adaptable
plant, native to Europe,
grows abundantly in
North America
along trails, roads,
creeks, streams,
riverbanks, and
in woods and
vacant lots.

Artemisia vulgaris

Mugwort, which has erect and branching stems, grows 6 inches to 5 feet tall. Its numerous, well-divided, highly aromatic leaves are a soft silver-green underneath and darker green on top. The spiked flower heads and seeds are densely clustered and also highly aromatic.

USAGE

- Mugwort has been used for centuries in Europe, China, and America.

- The name Mugwort is derived from its use as a flavoring agent in beers and ales, prior to the use of hops.

- Mugwort belongs to the Aster family, which includes the well-known Sagebrush varieties of the American West. Mugwort is closely related to tarragon and other wormwoods (formerly used to make the liqueur absinthe). The Japanese still use Mugwort for flavoring.

- You can gather leaves or entire plants from spring through autumn. The dried leaves have a strong flavor, and in small amounts, make an excellent seasoning.

- Nineteenth century American physicians prescribed Mugwort as a sedative, and it is still highly valued as an ingredient in traditional Chinese medicines.

- Hung on a wall or in small bundles over a door, fresh Mugwort plants emit a pleasant aroma as they dry. The dried plants make fine incense.

- A few cups of fresh, crushed leaves added to a hot bath are said to relieve aches.

A folk tale claims that placing Mugwort in your pillow brings dreams that reveal the future.

HABITAT

Native to Europe, Mullein grows throughout much of North America along roads and roadside ditches, in open fields and vacant lots, and in sunny patches along streams and rivers.

Verbascum thapsus

*A*lso known as *Candlewick*, this biennial appears in its first year as a ground–hugging rosette of large, oval– to–oblong, gray–green leaves. In its second year, Mullein develops a thick central flower stalk that grows 1 to 5 feet tall.

Throughout summer and autumn of the second year, numerous bright yellow flowers appear along the upper portion of the central stalk.

The entire plant is covered with fine hairs and appears furry or flannel–like.

U S A G E

❦ Mullein has been cultivated for centuries as a valuable medicine.

❦ A well-known treatment for earache calls for fresh Mullein flowers soaked in an equal amount of mineral or olive oil, strained, and used as eardrops.

❦ Mullein has long been used to treat lung disorders; the leaves, dried and smoked, are said to relieve asthma and lung congestion.

❦ A tea of crushed Mullein leaves can soothe coughs and hoarse throats. *Because the fine hairs of this plant can be irritating to the throat, Mullein tea should be poured through a fine strainer or cloth before drinking.*

❦ Traditionally, the large leaves, rolled and dried, were used as oil lamp wicks.

Fresh, soft Mullein leaves are a good, biodegradable substitute for toilet paper.

Wild Mustard

Brassica spp.

HABITAT

Wild Mustards grow along sidewalks, trails, and roadsides, and in vacant lots, open fields, and pastures.

Brassica campestris

*S*everal common Wild Mustard varieties grow throughout North America. These plants, with erect, branching stems, reach heights of 6 inches to 3 feet. All display small clusters of yellow, 4-petaled flowers.

The deeply lobed lower leaves, either smooth or bristly, are oblong to wide. Upper leaves are smaller.

Leaf edges vary from smooth to toothed or serrated.

Mustard plants' narrow seedpods grow erect from their stalks and contain many small seeds ranging in color from light brown to black. The pods ripen and dry from summer through autumn.

USAGE

❦ You can eat the young, tender greens raw, as well as the young flowers and flower buds. All are flavorful additions to other wild salad greens.

❦ Cook fresh leaves of any size in water until tender. Their strong flavor blends well with other wild greens that often grow nearby, such as Amaranth, Lamb's Quarters, Plantain, and Stinging Nettles.

❦ Gather the seeds, which can be ground for mustard, by rubbing the ripened dry seedpods between your fingers and allowing the small seeds to fall into a bag.

Wild Mustard
  – 2 Tbs. finely ground or powdered mustard seed
  – 2 Tbs. cider or other vinegar
  – 1 tsp. honey
  – Water to thin

Combine ground mustard seed and vinegar. Add honey (and a little water if the paste is too thick). If this mixture is too pungent, add a little acorn flour or other wild-seed or nut flour.

With this basic recipe, any combination of wild-food additives can be explored.
A few minced and sauteed wild onions are one possibility.

HABITAT

Stinging Nettles grow widely throughout North America, generally in damp or moist earth and often in shade. They grow in small to large patches near springs and wooded creeks.

Urtica dioica

*A*lso known as *Stinging Nettle* for the sharp sting it produces when brushed against or handled, this highly useful plant grows to 10 feet tall.

The mature, fine-haired leaves are roughly heart shaped, have serrated edges, and are 1 to 4 inches wide.

Small flowers droop in clusters at the junctions of erect stalks and leaf stems.

USAGE

❦ You can gather this plant from spring through autumn and year-round in some areas. Use a sharp knife or scissors and wear long sleeves and leather garden gloves.

❦ The young stems and leaves, and in some cases the older leaves, are delicious steamed or boiled. Mild flavored, the plant is good when added to other wild greens. *The irritating toxin that causes painful stings is completely neutralized by cooking the leaves.*

❦ You can harvest the mature stalks and stems of these plants and make them into strong thread or cordage *(see page 72)*. For centuries, nettle fibers have been woven into traditional fabrics. You can also incorporate these fibers into handmade paper *(see page 73)*.

❦ Dried leaves can be used throughout the year in soups, stews, and other dishes calling for cooked greens. The dry leaves also make a good hot tea, which resembles Japanese green tea.

Stinging Nettles contain valuable amounts of vitamins A and C and are high in iron.

H A B I T A T

Oak trees grow at different elevations in a variety of habitats, including street borders, open fields, dry plains, canyons, and foothills.

Quercus garryana

*N*orth American Oaks vary greatly in appearance from species to species. Many, for example, bear leaves that are simple in design on trees that are mostly shrublike. Other varieties grow to great heights and produce more complex foliage, with leaves well divided or deeply lobed. There are deciduous varieties and species that remain green year-round.

One feature common to all Oaks is their usually 1-seeded nut, the acorn.

U S A G E

* Acorns have been a human food staple for thousands of years. They are important food for many wild animals, too. Traditionally, people have gathered these highly nutritious nuts in great quantities each autumn and stored them for use throughout the following seasons.

* Acorns contain tannin, which can be quite bitter. Before they are eaten, acorns generally need to be leached. The following method is one of several.

To remove bitter tannin
- Soak acorns in warm water for 20 to 30 minutes, discarding any that float.
- Drain water and remove shells with a nutcracker or by cracking each nut, on end, with a stone.
- Grind or finely chop the nutmeats
- Place the acorn meal in a strainer or piece of clean cloth and run hot or boiling water through it until clear or until the nuts are free of bitterness.
- Leaching can also be done by placing the nut meal in a cloth sack and submerging it in the moving water of a creek or river. This process takes approximately 1 to 3 days.

Nutritious and flavorful acorn meal can be used in a variety of ways (see pages 75–76).

Wild Onion

Allium spp.

HABITAT

These plants are widely distributed throughout North America in vacant lots, plains, deserts, foothills, woodlands, brooksides, and mountain meadows.

Allium cernuum

*N*umerous species of Wild Onion grow throughout North America and range in height from several inches to 2 1/2 feet.

In spring and summer, beautiful flowers framed by narrow leaves appear in clusters at the ends of erect stalks. These flowers come in a wide range of colors, including white, pink, rose, and purple.

The bulbs, leaves, and stalks all smell and taste of onion or garlic.

U S A G E

❦ Native peoples have valued Wild Onions for centuries. In fact, the city of Chicago derives its name from the beautiful plants that once grew abundantly in that area, now covered by city streets.

❦ Use Wild Onions as you would commercial varieties. Bulbs and greens are delicious when fresh or can be dried easily and stored for later use. Bulbs of any size can be pickled. You can make delicious soup or stew using Wild Onions and any variety of the edible plants listed in this book.

❦ Dig bulbs with a small shovel or hand trowel throughout spring and summer.

❦ Wild Onions are rich in vitamins A, B, and C, iron, and calcium.

❦ Skins of numerous species make a range of natural dyes *(see page 74).*

☞ *Caution: The poisonous Death Camas is somewhat similar in appearance to certain species of Wild Onions. If the plant does not smell like onion or garlic, do not eat it.*

H A B I T A T

*P*lantain grows along roadsides and sidewalks, and in fields and vacant lots.

Plantago major

*T*he lower leaves of two species of Plantain common to North America stem from basal rosettes. *Major* has oval to round leaves, 2 to 8 inches long. *Lanceolata* has longer, narrower leaves.

Flowers and seeds of both varieties appear in spiked clusters at the tops of straight, narrow stalks that are several inches to 2 feet tall.

U S A G E

- ❧ Historically, the Chinese have used Plantain as food. The seeds of this valuable, and now common, wild plant have also been discovered in the tombs of Egyptian pharaohs.

- ❧ Very young leaves are best for eating, since they're the most tender. They can be eaten raw in salads and are also good steamed or lightly boiled.

- ❧ Older leaves, with their stringy fibers removed, are best cooked until tender.

- ❧ Mature Plantain produces abundant tiny seeds in clusters along narrow stalks. These seed stalks can be collected easily by clipping them off at their bases. The cleaned and roasted seeds can be used in a variety of ways *(see pages 75-76)*.

- ❧ Medicinally, the raw whole seeds act as a laxative.

Plantain seeds contain high amounts of valuable oil and are a favorite food of many wild birds. You can easily bundle together the mature seed stalks and use them as natural bird feeders.

Prickly Lettuce

Lactua serriola

HABITAT

Prickly Lettuce has adapted to a wide range of environments, including open fields, vacant lots, and along sidewalks, roadsides, garden walls, and fences.

Lactua serriola

*P*rickly Lettuce, also known as *Compass Plant*, grows abundantly throughout North America, reaching a height of 3 to 4 feet.

The lower leaves are generally the largest, with or without deep lobes or notches and, like the smaller upper leaves, tightly clasp the erect and branching stems. Prickles line the midribs and sometimes the edges of the largest leaves.

The small yellow flowers resemble Dandelions and become fluffy white seed heads when mature.

USAGE

* This abundant plant is the ancestor of today's cultivated lettuces eaten worldwide. In fact, most garden lettuces strongly resemble wild Prickly Lettuce if allowed to go to seed.

* The young leaves of this valuable plant are good in salads but become bitter with age; therefore, they are best cooked when mature. The older leaves may require a change of water once or twice while cooking, and are especially good with a little butter and vinegar.

* Prickly Lettuce, cultivated for centuries as food, has also been medically important. American doctors of the nineteenth century considered the sap of Prickly Lettuce to be a valuable nonnarcotic substitute for opium; it was used, to some degree, for this purpose.

Roman Emperor Augustus believed that a medicine derived from lettuce saved his life. He erected an altar and statue in honor of the plant.

H A B I T A T

urslane, widespread throughout North America, often grows
at lower elevations in cultivated or disturbed ground. It flourishes along
sidewalks and roadsides and in gardens.

Portulaca oleracea

*T*he small, succulent, fleshy leaves of this low-growing plant spread in large numbers along numerous branches of ground-running stems.

Small yellow flowers and tiny black seeds appear in clusters along reddish stems 2 to 12 inches long.

U S A G E

❦ You can gather purslane year-round in some areas, and from spring through autumn in many other regions.

❦ Add the tart leaves and stems to salads, or try them steamed, baked, or lightly sautéed. These greens can be used to thicken any variety of soup or stew. The entire plant is often gritty from growing close to the ground and generally needs a thorough rinsing.

❦ Purslane stems cut to any size are good pickled.

❦ Gather the tiny seeds, a valuable food for many wild birds, by shaking the plants over an open box or bag. They make an excellent buckwheatlike flour when lightly roasted and ground *(see pages 75-76)*.

❦ By pinching off just what is needed for each meal, you will help these delicious plants produce an abundance of new stems and leaves throughout the season.

Commercially grown in many countries, including the United States, Purslane is high in iron. It is popular in some Mexican markets, where it is known as Verdolaga.

HABITAT

Introduced from Europe, Red Clover grows abundantly throughout North America in a variety of moist, and occasionally dry, habitats.

Trifolium pratense

*R*ed Clover leaves are oval to oblong and grow in groups of 3 or occasionally 4 to 5. A characteristic whitish V shape marks each leaflet.

The multiple, branching stems grow 6 inches to 3 feet high, with numerous flower heads ranging from pink to magenta to red-purple.

U S A G E

❦ You can eat Red Clover roots, leaves, flowers, and seeds. Add the tender young leaves raw to salads; cook the older leaves, flowers, and seeds to make them more digestible.

❦ Sauté, steam, or boil the roots and leaves and eat plain, or add to other dishes of wild greens, including soups and stews.

❦ Add the flowers and seeds to baked goods, or, like the leaves and roots of the plant, use them fresh or dried in soups and stews.

❦ Red Clover blossoms are used to make a soothing syrup for sore throats and coughs. Fresh or dried, they make an excellent hot tea.

Clover Syrup
- Combine 4 cups of gently crushed clover blossoms with 1 $^1/_2$ cups honey and 1 $^1/_2$ cups water.
- Bring to a boil slowly, reduce heat, and simmer uncovered 10 to 20 minutes.
- Cool, strain, and bottle.

Red Clover, high in protein, has long been used
for making a good spring tonic.

Wild Rose

Rosa spp.

H A B I T A T

Wild Roses grow at
various elevations and in a
wide range of habitats
including along
creeks, streams,
rivers, canyons,
and hillsides, and
in open fields,
woodlands, and
moist mountain
meadows.

Rosa sp.

*W*ild Rose grows as a bush or shrub 3 to 9 feet tall. Its numerous small, oval, serrated leaflets grow opposite each other along single stems.

In spring and summer, delicate, usually 5-petaled flowers appear in colors ranging from white to yellow to pink and rose-red.

Most of the species in this genus have thorns or prickles, but some do not.

Small, bright orange or red fruits, called hips, ripen in autumn. A frost or cold snap will generally intensify their color and flavor.

U S A G E

* When dried, the leaves, flowers, and hips make good tea, and can be added to other wild-tea blends as well. The fresh flower petals are a nice addition to salads.

* Remove the seeds of the fresh or dried fruits by simmering the hips in just enough water to cover, and allow to cook down to a soft, juicy pulp. Strain the stewed hips and use the strained liquid in jams, jellies, syrups, and other foods.

* You can grind dried rosehips into a vitamin-rich powder and add to any number of foods and drinks. (Some species have seeds small enough to be ground in with the dried fruit, but others may require seed removal.)

* Rosehips are rich in iron and vitamin C.

Rosebuds are a good addition to dried-flower arrangements, and the delicate flower petals can be used for making rose water.

Sheep Sorrel

Rumex acetosella

HABITAT

*S*heep Sorrel is common along sidewalks and roadsides, and in fields, vacant lots, and moist woodland soils.

Rumex acetosella

*T*he largest leaves of Sheep Sorrel grow near the base of the plant, are oval to oblong, and have a characteristic arrowhead or lancelike shape. In general, the upper leaves are smaller and simpler in design.

Flowers and seeds appear in clusters along slender, branching stalks 4 to 24 inches tall.

USAGE

- This abundant and lovely plant from Europe has long been appreciated as a valuable and delicious food. As a medicinal herb, it has been used to treat skin problems.

- Sheep Sorrel leaves are tender when cooked and have a pleasant sour quality. They are good mixed with milder tasting foods. You can also use the raw young leaves in salads.

- Sorrel makes delicious soup.

Sheep Sorrel Soup

- 4 cups chopped nettle leaves *(or other wild greens)*
- 4 cups chopped sorrel greens
- 1 cup chopped wild onions
- Cow parsnip ash to season *(see page 18)*

Sauté wild onions in a small amount of oil or butter, or simmer slowly in just enough water to cover, for 5 to 10 minutes.

Add chopped greens, cover with water, and simmer gently until greens are tender.

Season to taste with cow parsnip ash or salt.

For thicker soup, blend in a little wild-seed or acorn flour *(see pages 75-76)*.

Sheep Sorrel is safe to eat in moderate amounts, but contains oxalic acid, which can be harmful to some people if consumed in large quantities.

HABITAT

*T*his common plant grows in or at the edges of open fields and vacant lots, along sidewalks and road-sides, and in a wide variety of dry habitats.

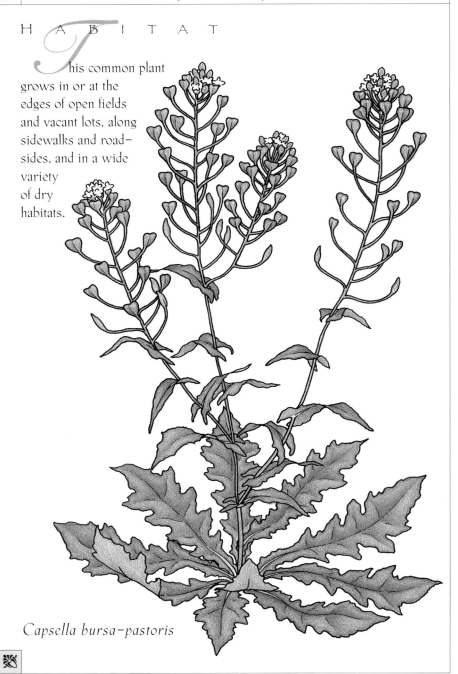

Capsella bursa-pastoris

*S*hepherd's Purse grows 4 to 24 inches tall, with its main stem rising from a rosette of oblong and deep-lobed, or deeply toothed, leaves.

The upper leaves are much smaller and generally free of notches or lobes.

Delicate, 4-petaled white flowers appear in clusters at the tips of stalks, eventually forming tiny, heart-shaped seedpods borne at the ends of small, straight stems.

USAGE

- You can gather Shepherd's Purse from spring through autumn and year-round in many areas.

- Young leaves are good raw in salads; older leaves are best steamed or boiled.

- The seeds ripen in summer and autumn and can often be gathered in substantial numbers. They are good roasted *(see pages 75-76)*.

- The dried roots have a gingerlike flavor, making them a valuable wild-food seasoning.

- Shepherd's Purse is high in vitamins A and C and contains vitamin K, an important aid in blood clotting.

The seedpods of this often abundant wild plant resemble leather purses worn by shepherds in the Old World.

Sow Thistle

Sonchus oleraceus

HABITAT

*T*hese plants grow along sidewalks, roadsides, and trails, and in fields and vacant lots, gardens, and open woodlands.

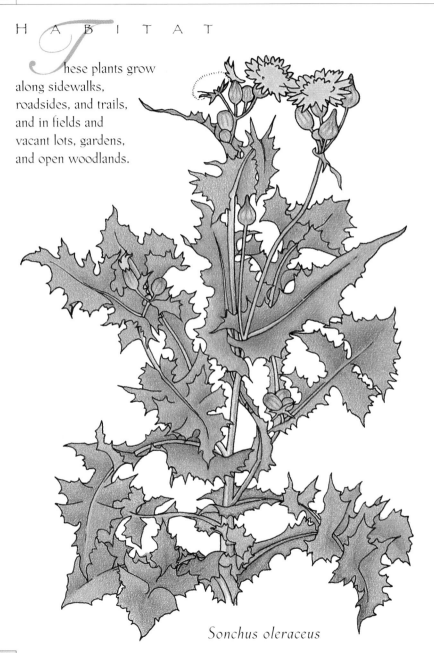

Sonchus oleraceus

*S*ow Thistle grows 1 to 6 feet tall and has hollow, branching stems that exude a milky sap when broken.

The oblong, deeply lobed lower leaves clasp the stems and have irregular teeth along their edges. The upper leaves, generally less defined, are usually smaller.

Yellow, dandelion-like flowers are often numerous on individual plants in spring and summer, becoming delicate white seed-puffs when mature.

USAGE

❧ Sow Thistle, introduced from Europe, grows abundantly throughout North America and has been a valued plant for centuries. Greeks and Romans used the milklike sap to treat eye and skin problems. The sap and leaves have also been important ingredients in traditional Chinese medicine.

❧ Sow Thistle's tender young leaves, although strong in flavor, are a good addition to salads, soups, stews, and dishes calling for cooked greens.

❧ These greens often become bitter with age and may need to be cooked in one or two changes of fresh water.

House finches enjoy the seeds of Sow Thistle, while hummingbirds collect the soft down from the flower heads of mature plants.

Wild Strawberry

Fragaria spp.

HABITAT

*T*hese plants grow throughout North America in moist woodlands, along paths and trails, on sunny hillsides, and in mountain fields and meadows.

Fragaria vesca

*E*xcept for their smaller fruits and leaves, Wild Strawberries closely resemble the larger, cultivated varieties.

Serrated, oval, pointed leaves emerge from running stems.

Delicate white to pink flowers appear in early spring.

The 2 most common species of Wild Strawberry in North America are *F. vesca* and *F. virginiana*.

USAGE

❦ You can often find Wild Strawberries in abundance, with fruit ripening in late spring or early summer.

❦ The fruit is the essence of strawberry. Many consider it much finer in flavor than cultivated commercial varieties.

❦ The dried or fresh leaves make an excellent tea or addition to wild-tea blends.

❦ Compared with commercial varieties, the berries are quite small. Under favorable conditions, you can gather enough of this precious fruit to make preserves, tarts, pies, and other dishes.

❦ You can easily dry the berries and store them for later use in pancakes, muffins, and other baked goods.

❦ These berries are a valuable source of niacin, thiamin, and vitamin C. Tea made from the leaves is said to benefit the kidneys.

A Wild Strawberry pie or tart with a crust of blended wild flours (including Hazelnut) is just one of many tasty ways to use this special fruit.

Wild Sunflower

Helianthus annuus

HABITAT

Wild Sunflowers grow along roads and ditches, on hillsides, and in vacant lots, open fields, canyons, deserts, plains, and meadows.

Helianthus annuus

*T*hroughout summer and early autumn, you can see Wild Sunflowers' many distinctive brown-centered, yellow-petaled flower heads, which are borne on numerous, branching stems.

The dull green leaves have coarsely toothed edges and are oval to oval-triangular.

This beautiful plant grows to 9 feet tall and is often covered with fine hairs or soft prickles.

USAGE

❧ Many species belonging to the Aster family have delicious, highly nutritious seeds.

❧ As well as being beautiful, the common Wild Sunflower has great nutritional value.

❧ The small seeds, which ripen in summer and autumn, provide a rich source of oil and protein. Often, they can be gathered in great quantities.

❧ Collect the seeds by rubbing mature flower heads between your hands or fingers (use gloves if you like), allowing the dry seeds to fall into a bag or box. This can be done while the flower heads are still on the drying plant; or, snip off the heads and remove the seeds later.

❧ The seed-meats are small and can be difficult to separate from their shells. One simple method is to chop the seeds coarsely, by hand or in a grinder, and immerse in water. The meats should sink as the shell pieces float.

❧ Eat the seeds raw or roasted, or grind into a useful flour *(see pages 75-76)*. They are excellent in baked goods and other cooked dishes.

Wild Sunflowers can be used for making paper (see page 73).
The flower petals make a yellow dye (see page 74).

Thistle

Cirsium spp. (and other closely related species)

H A B I T A T

Thistles grow throughout North America in woodlands, open fields, meadows, and vacant lots, along roads and trails, and on dry hillsides.

Silybum marianum

A wide variety of common Thistles (most of the genus *Cirsium*) grow from 6 inches to 8 feet high. Sharp-toothed, spiny, needle-edged leaves grow to 10 inches long.

Neatly trimmed, brushlike flower heads come in a variety of sizes and colors, including white, pink, red, and purple.

USAGE

❦ You can harvest thistles as food from spring through autumn, or year-round in some regions.

❦ Eat the peeled young stalks and stems of any common Thistle raw or cooked. The cleaned roots can be boiled, steamed, roasted, or eaten raw. Young leaves, with their spikes trimmed off, are good when cooked until tender.

❦ Some thistle species have large flower heads that can be boiled or steamed and eaten like artichokes, also in the Aster family. Compared to artichokes, the leaf and heart-meats of Wild Thistles are much smaller. They can be worth the effort, though.

❦ In many areas, it's possible to gather large quantities of thistle seeds, generally in summer and autumn, when the flower heads begin to dry. Shake the dry flower heads into a sturdy bag or box, and separate the seeds from the fluffy down.

❦ These seeds can be roasted and used for making flour *(see pages 75-76)* or as an ingredient in teas or other beverages. Try brewing the roasted and ground seeds with roasted Chicory or Dandelion root for a good coffee substitute.

❦ As herbal medicines, all thistles are said to benefit the liver, especially the Milk Thistle *(Silybum marianum)*.

Wear heavy gloves and long sleeves when collecting thistles.

H A B I T A T

*T*hese lovely plants grow in a wide range of habitats, including lowlands and mountains.

Although able to grow in dry or damp earth, they do well in moist and shady environments, including woodlands and near creeks and streams.

Viola adunca

*W*ild Violets vary in size, shape, and color, depending on species and habitat. In general, they grow low to the ground in small to large patches, with roughly heart–shaped and often tooth–edged leaves.

The delicate flowers bloom in shades of white, yellow, pink, blue, or violet.

USAGE

❦ The blossoms, leaves, and stems of Wild Violets and of most cultivated varieties are edible.

❦ The young leaves and flowers, which bloom from early spring through autumn, are a delicious and beautiful addition to salads.

❦ Use the leaves, fresh or dried, to thicken soups and stews. This use has earned Wild Violets the nickname *Wild Okra* in some areas. The dried leaves are also used for making tea or as an ingredient in wild-tea blends.

❦ The flowers can be candied or used to make flavored vinegar.

Wild Violet Vinegar

- Fill a jar of any size with Wild Violet flowers.
- Cover entirely with white vinegar.
- Cap and store for one month.
- Strain into bottles.

These plants are an excellent source of vitamins A and C.
Rabbits and wild birds eat the seeds.

HABITAT

*W*illows usually indicate the presence of water and are often found near springs, irrigation ditches, creeks, streams, and rivers.

Salix sp.

*N*umerous species of Willow throughout North America include varieties unique to specific habitats or regions.

In general, Willows have smooth, short–stemmed leaves that are narrow or lancelike.

Soft, fuzzy, spikelike flower clusters known as catkins are borne on branches along with new leaves in the spring. The ripe seeds of mature flower heads are often carried by wind, aiding distribution.

The bark of Willows is smooth or wrinkled and comes in a range of colors: gray, blackish gray, light to dark brown, and shades of yellow and green.

These valuable shrubs and trees grow from bush size to 40 feet tall.

U S A G E

❧ Humans have valued Willows for countless generations.

❧ The strong, flexible wood of these trees is still used by many indigenous peoples for making sturdy, beautiful baskets, as well as providing lightweight strength for items such as cradleboards.

❧ Willows grow easily from cuttings and make good, fast growing windbreaks. In some rural areas, rows of mature Willows are actually former fence posts that rooted and grew.

❧ Medicinally, Willow is said to act like its modern chemical counterpart, aspirin. Traditionally, a strong tea made from the dried bark or twigs has relieved headaches and reduced fever. On larger trees, young, smooth bark provides the most potent medicine, while on bushlike Willows, the darker stems are of greater value.

The wide variety of Willow barks are a good source
of natural dyes (see page 74).

*H*ere are a few important things to consider when collecting wild plants:

❧ *Be mindful of your surroundings.*

Public roadways are often sprayed with herbicides, and heavily traveled roads are subjected to high levels of automotive pollutants. Avoid plants in such areas.

In general, if plants appear clean, healthy, and strong, they are probably safe to use. If you are uncertain about the toxicity of any habitat, *do not* use plants from that environment.

❧ *Respect habitats.*

Many plant communities include rare and endangered species. Therefore, it is important to collect only wild plants that are growing in healthy numbers, and to leave enough for an individual species to continue in any given area. This is especially true in more natural or wild habitats. To the extent possible, avoid disrupting the biodiversity of the plant community.

❧ *Be certain of identification.*

Many wild plants, particularly in their early stages of development, are not easy to recognize. Collect and use only those plants you can identify positively.

A Basic Tool Kit for Collecting

- A heavy canvas bag
- Paper and/or plastic bags
- Small garden shears
- Scissors
- A sharp pocketknife
- Heavy cotton or leather work gloves
- Long-sleeved shirt
- A small shovel or garden trowel

*M*any of the plants in this book can be dried for later use. Here are a few basic steps to help with this process.

Drying

In general, most whole fresh plants, or parts of plants, dry well when they are hung upside down and allowed to age slowly, away from moisture, direct heat, and sunlight.

The roots of many plants can be dried by placing them on a piece of wood or screen, thick paper or cloth, and turning them over from time to time. Small roots can easily be dried whole this way. Cut larger roots lengthwise into sections before drying. These roots or root sections can be bundled together at one end and hung to dry.

Place berries and other fruits on a piece of screen, paper, or wood and dry in more direct heat and sunlight. A very low-temperature oven or food dehydrator also achieves good results.

Flowers and flower clusters should be dried slowly, away from direct sunlight.

Storage

Once the drying process is complete, whole plants or plant parts can be broken or chopped into smaller sections and stored for later use.

Tightly covered glass jars or earthenware containers are good for storing dried plants and should be kept away from direct heat and sunlight.

*N*umerous wild plants, including at least a handful mentioned in this book, contain valuable fibers that can be used in a variety of ways. Traditionally, plant fibers have been employed in the making of such items as baskets, cordage, fabrics, and paper.

Follow these steps to obtain useful fibers from the often abundant Stinging Nettle plant *(see page 38)*.

To Render Fibers from Stinging Nettles

- Collect dry, older plants in late summer or autumn. *(Remember to wear gloves throughout this entire process.)*

- Dry single main stalks thoroughly in a hot, sunny place. (The back of a car with the windows rolled up works well.)

- Quarter the dried stalks into long divisions by cracking them apart with a stone or other blunt tool.

- Allow the quartered sections to dry further in a hot, sunny spot.

- When they are completely dry, gently pound and bend the stalk sections, separating the outermost bark from the central woody interior. (The fine, long fibers are the valuable element and are part of this outer skin or bark.)

- Vigorously rub the lengths of outer skin between the palms of your hands. This process should separate the darker bark from the lighter, valuable inner fibers.

   These fibers can now be braided or woven into a strong thread, string, or other binding material. A fine fabric can also be woven from Stinging Nettles, and the fibers of the fresh, green plants are useful in handmade papers as well.

*T*here are many detailed papermaking books available. The following recipe is basic, but will work well with fibers of the Stinging Nettle (see *page 58*) and Wild Sunflower (see *page 62*). Many other wild plants contain usable fibers. These instructions can be used as a basis for experimenting.

To Make a Simple Paper from Natural Fibers

- Cut fresh, green stalks (or fibrous leaves) into 1/4- to 1/2-inch lengths.

- Cover with lye water (1 Tbs. lye per 1 qt. water) and boil to a soft mush, approximately 15 to 20 minutes, or in some cases a bit longer. *(Lye causes serious burns to eyes and skin, so proceed with caution. Wear gloves and safety glasses.)*

- Rinse entire mixture in a strainer. The tougher plant fibers are the essential element in papermaking, but any amount of less fibrous pulp that remains after rinsing can produce interesting effects.

- Add equal parts of fiber pulp and water and mix in a covered electric blender, using no more than a cup or two of this mixture at a time.

- Cut a piece of window screen to lie flat in a rectangular or square pan or tub, then fill with 3 to 5 inches of water.

- Pour 2 to 4 cups of blended pulp into the pan. (The more pulp, the thicker the paper.)

- Spread the pulp around and mix it evenly into the water with your fingers.

- Carefully lift out the screen, keeping it as level as possible. (Tacking the screen onto a simple wooden framework helps.)

- Place the screen, pulp side up, on several sheets of newspaper.

(continued on next page)

- Place a few sheets of newspaper or pages from an old phone book onto the pulp–mixture side of the screen.

- Using a flat piece of wood, press down evenly on the paper to remove as much water as possible from the pulp.

- Gently lift the newspaper away from the screen.

- The plant–paper will most likely adhere to the wet newspaper and should be allowed to dry somewhat before separating. (If desired, this natural paper can be pressed while still slightly damp to achieve a somewhat smoother texture.)

P L A N T   D Y E S

*N*atural dyes in an array of lovely hues can be extracted from wild plants. This ancient process is quite simple.

Use all parts of any given plant to obtain natural dyes. This includes roots, leaves, barks, flowers, seeds, and fruits.

Dyeing with plants is not an exact science. The same plant produces different results depending on fabric and color fixative used. Also, dye colors are often quite different from the colors of the plant itself.

The following instructions work best with wool, or sometimes cotton, although these two fibers or fabrics generally produce very different results using the same plant dye. Wool is preferred, but try any natural fiber. Remember, this is a process of experimentation.

To Dye Natural Fibers with Plant Extracts

- Wash material with a mild, nondetergent soap, rinse in warm water, and dry.

- Chop whole plants or plant parts into pieces, cover with $1\frac{1}{2}$ to 2 gallons of water, and soak for several hours. Berries should be gently crushed first. Roots should be finely chopped and soaked overnight. Soft water or rainwater is preferred. In general, the more plant material you use, the more intense the dye.

- Combine 1 ½ Tbs. potassium alum (available in drugstores) and ½ Tbs. cream of tartar (available in grocery stores). Blend with 1 cup of boiling water and add to approximately 2 gallons of warm water in a large pot or kettle. This mixture mordants or permanently fixes the color to the material. Different chemical mordants produce a range of natural colors.

- Dampen material with warm water, place it in the pot or kettle, and bring slowly to a simmer. Do not boil, but continue to simmer gently for 1 hour.

- Remove from heat and allow fabric bath to cool.

- In a separate pot or kettle, bring the soaking plant/water mixture to a boil and simmer 1 to 1 ½ hours. Cool until warm, and strain out the plant material.

- Add the damp, premordanted material to the warm dye bath, and bring slowly to a boil.

- Reduce heat and simmer 20 to 45 minutes, or until desired color is achieved.

N U T S   A N D   S E E D S

*M*any wild plants produce edible seeds and nuts. Discovering, collecting, and using these wild foods requires patience and practice.

The following basic steps for using seeds and nuts of wild plants apply to a number of plants mentioned in this book.

About Seeds

- The majority of seed and nut plants are ready for harvesting in summer and autumn.

(continued on next page)

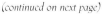

- In general, you can collect edible seeds by shaking the mature flowers or flower heads into a bag, box, or basket. Rubbing the flowers between your fingers or hands may also be necessary.

- Lightly roasting or parching collected seeds in a low–heat oven (200° F or less) for 10 to 20 minutes often increases their flavor and aids in winnowing or removing the outer husks or chaff.

- To remove the chaff from parched or roasted seeds, rub the seeds between your hands or fingers, allowing the heavier seed–meats to fall into a container.

- Using a pie pan or wide–rimmed bowl, gently toss the seeds a few inches into the air in a series of regular, even motions, allowing any excess chaff to be carried off in the breeze.

- Further roasting of the cleaned seeds often intensifies their flavor.

About Seed and Nut Flours

- Cleaned and roasted nuts and seeds can be ground into useful and delicious flours. A coffee grinder or electric blender will work, but a hand–operated gristmill produces the finest results. Find these compact, easy–to–use mills at many hardware, cookware, and natural food stores.

- You can use wild–seed and nut flours in breads, biscuits, cakes, and pancakes, and to thicken soups and stews. They can also be used in cookies and pie crusts.

- Cook wild–plant seeds, whole, ground, raw, or roasted, in water to make hot cereal. Eat as is, or dry in the sun or a low–temperature oven and use as flour.

- As with a number of roasted roots, some dark–roasted seeds and seed husks can be used for brewing coffeelike beverages.